The Launch Lens

THE
Launch
Lens

TWENTY QUESTIONS EVERY
ENTREPRENEUR SHOULD ASK

Jim Price

Faculty and Entrepreneur in Residence
Zell Lurie Institute for Entrepreneurial Studies
Ross School of Business
University of Michigan

Published in the United States of America by
Michigan Publishing

ISBN 978-1-60785-476-0 (paper)
ISBN 978-1-60785-477-7 (e-book)

Contents

Exhibits

Dedicated to my father, William H. Price,
inventor of the original zoom lens

Introduction

I'll frequently start off a workshop or talk asking for a show of hands: "How many of you have thought of a new-business idea—in the shower or at the kitchen table, during your commute, while chatting with friends and colleagues—and said to yourself, 'Man, if somebody did this, they'd be rich'?" Most everyone's hand shoots up, and I see knowing smiles and nods. For many, Americans in particular, this sort of entrepreneurial musing seems almost a universal condition.

I'll then ask, "OK, so how do you follow up on your ideas?" And the all-too-frequent response is, "I Google it, discover one or more companies are already pursuing this idea or something awfully close, and sadly conclude, 'My idea's taken.'"

It's at that point that I'll offer my thesis that there's no such thing as an original business idea, and that execution—not the idea itself but how it's implemented—is everything. With all the smart people in this world, this thesis goes, if you come upon a really good product or service idea, you can't tell me that someone, somewhere, hasn't already thought about it (or isn't already actively pursuing it). Therefore, if you do a search of your business concept and discover others already pursuing it, rather than saying to yourself, "Darn, my idea's already taken," perhaps a more appropriate reaction would be, "Fantastic—market validation!" (The converse might also be true: if you search for your business idea and can't find anything, that too might be a clue—an indication that there may be no market for your product or service concept.)

What's struck me over the years as I've mentored entrepreneurs, taught thousands of MBAs and undergrads, and advised corporations on launching new businesses and products is how often smart people will come up with new business concepts and then simply stop. They're good at the gee-whiz brainstorming, but then they stall out, unclear about how to take the idea to the next level.

It's with that in mind that I created the Launch Lens, a framework for articulating, comparing, and screening new-business concepts. Comprising a series of twenty common-sense questions, the framework equips individuals with a way of viewing the world that, once applied a few times, can be internalized to provide you with an improved "startup-idea lens": a consistent way of screening and evaluating new-business concepts as they cross your field of vision.

Exhibit A lists the twenty questions, or Focal Points, comprising the Launch Lens framework.

Its flexibility makes the Launch Lens broadly applicable in a variety of settings. The tool is useful for the following:

- **Aspiring entrepreneurs**—The framework enables anyone contemplating a startup to document, catalog, and screen new ideas as they come to mind as well as compare their relative appeal and viability.
- **Early-stage startups**—Your entrepreneurial team can make sure you're clearly articulating your business in order to (a) make sure everyone's on the same page and (b) communicate the idea to others.
- **Innovators in established companies**—Product managers, new-business development teams, innovation groups, and new-product launch teams can rack and stack alternative ideas and approaches and make apples-to-apples comparisons.

EXHIBIT A

THE LAUNCH LENS: 20-QUESTION ENTREPRENEURSHIP FRAMEWORK

Problem	1. Who are your customers?
	2. What is your customers' unmet need?
	3. How are your customers addressing this need today?
Solution	4. What is your solution?
	5. How will your customers benefit?
Market	6. How big is your market?
	7. Which customer segments will you target, and why?
	8. Who are your competitors, and how do you compare?
Business model	9. How will your business make money?
	10. How will you price your product?
	11. Which functions will you perform in-house vs. outsource?
	12. How scalable is your business?
Marketing and sales	13. How will you gather customer input?
	14. How will your customers acquire your product?
	15. How will you promote to your customers?
Finance	16. How much will it cost to launch the business?
	17. Can the business generate sustainably high profits?
	18. At what point could you quit your day job?
Capital	19. Is outside funding appropriate, and from whom would you raise it?
Team	20. Do you have the right team?

- **Startup investors**—Individual angel investors, angel groups, and venture capitalists have a consistent framework to compare and contrast alternative investments.
- **Incubators and accelerators**—Startup launch pads and accelerator services now have a way to coach their client entrepreneurs through a consistent framework for evaluating, articulating, and communicating their startup concepts.
- **Nonprofits**—Nonprofits, health care institutions, and NGOs are frequently looking to develop new service offerings or enter new markets or geographies; this tool enables them to more rigorously develop and document their ideas for internal and board communications as well as fundraising.

As you get practice applying the Launch Lens to screen, compare, and communicate various new business ideas, you're likely to find that it becomes ingrained, enabling you to filter ideas at various levels of detail and speed, ranging from the following:

- **A twenty-minute screen**—For getting a quick gauge on whether a business idea even makes sense: Is there even a market? Why should customers care? Is there a way to make money?
- **A five-hour screen**—For concepts that pass your initial screen and merit further exploration, including, for instance, an extensive internet search.
- **A five-day screen**—For new business ideas that are stronger still and call for research and analysis to develop more rigorous answers to the various questions of the Launch Lens.

The chapters of this book "zoom in" on each of the twenty Focal Point questions of the Launch Lens, providing explanatory details and useful tips. The Focal Points are logically grouped by business topic in the following sequence:

- problem
- solution
- market
- business model
- marketing and sales
- finance
- capital
- team

In the back of the book, you'll find a useful Launch Lens Work-sheet to copy and use to your heart's content. Happy venturing!

I

THE PROBLEM

Conceptualizing any new business starts by articulating a clear problem statement. Exactly what is the problem or market need that you hope to address? By developing concise answers to the first three Focal Points of the Launch Lens, you'll find that you have clearly articulated your problem statement.

CHAPTER 1

Who Are Your Customers?

What we mean by the question "Who are your customers?" is to ask you to *generically describe the types of customers* (not to list your specific customers).

That is, what are the categories of consumers, businesses, or other entities that will purchase and use your product or service? If you have a consumer product, is your target market Hispanic preteen girls in Southern California . . . or Baby Boomer men and women throughout North America . . . or music lovers over thirty with disposable incomes of $35,000 or more . . . or who? Be as clear as possible.

If you have a business-to-business (B2B) product, is your target market small retail establishments, big-box retail chains, warehouse operators, software developers, or who? And importantly, with B2B customers, you need to specify not just the type of enterprise that would use your product or service but the job description of the individual who would be the typical user. Would the end user be a warehouse manager or a forklift operator? A chief engineer or a designer? A clinic director, a physician's assistant, or a billing specialist?

And if the end users are different from the economic buyers, it's important to note that. For instance, end users for educational software apps might be schoolchildren, but the economic buyers may be a combination of school districts and parents. End users of meals in rest homes are probably the elderly residents, whereas the economic buyers may be the institution or perhaps the adult children of the elderly residents. End users of business intelligence software might be various individuals within a corporation's staff function, while the economic buyer could be the CFO.

 TIPS

- Characterize types of customers rather than listing actual customers.
- When you're describing the types of customers, be specific. For instance, if your product is a football-oriented mobile game catering to eighteen- to twenty-four-year-old "gamer" males, say so; stating your customers include anyone with a mobile phone is so broad and nonspecific as to be unhelpful. If you're in the restaurant supply business and provide fresh spices for Indian-cuisine establishments, say so; describing your customers as including anyone who eats, or all restaurants, is too broad.

 RED FLAGS

- Avoid being too sweeping or general. If you're establishing a building supply store in Elyria, Ohio, saying that your customers are all US homeowners and contractors is not helpful; describing your customers as DIY homeowners and contractors in Lorain County and the western suburbs of Cleveland would be more accurate.

- Avoid being too narrow: the common urge is to describe your target customers as only those people just like you. Is your career-advice app only helpful for MBAs from top-ten schools (because that's your perspective), or is it useful for two-year and four-year college grads, grad school candidates, and mid-career changers?

CHAPTER 2

What Is Your Customers' Unmet Need?

To pose this question in another way, What is the customers' "pain" that your product or service is designed to ameliorate or address? (You'll be describing your product or service a bit later, in Focal Point #4.) This could be an acute or dramatic unmet need—for instance, for the inventors of the pacemaker, the customers' unmet need was that their hearts were beating slowly or unpredictably, thereby endangering their lives. On the other hand, for some businesses, the unmet need might be less of a need than a want—for instance, for the founders of a business producing hand-sewn, leather-bound journals, the "unmet need" might simply be the desire on the part of some writers, diarists, and office workers for a more personal, unique notebook.

TIPS

- Generally speaking, you'll encounter greater customer demand for your new product to the extent that it's addressing a more burning need. So ask yourself, would your solution be solving a "shark-bite pain" (your target customers *must have* this solution) or more of a "mosquito-bite pain" (it'd be *nice to have* your solution but not critical)?

RED FLAGS

- Be sure not to overstate the customers' unmet need; be honest.
- If you're struggling to articulate a clear and compelling unmet need, that's a clue that your target customers may not need or want your new product or service.

CHAPTER 3

How Are Your Customers Addressing This Need Today?

Even if your business has a novel way of addressing a customer need, remember that *those customers were addressing that need in some other fashion before you came along*. Before Henry Ford introduced the Model T, the vast majority of his target customers were not driving cars, and yet those people were already addressing their transportation needs through some combination of walking, horse-drawn buggy, and train. Before the advent of the cell phone, individuals got along with a combination of landlines at home, in their offices, and in phone booths (you can find them all in old movies). Before SMS texting, people got by with email. Before email, people made due with phone calls, postal mail, and faxes.

TIPS

- If you feel that you have a novel way of addressing a particular customer need, you may not have direct competitors for your product. In that case, you may need to look for indirect competitors—solutions or methods that your target customers are currently using to address that need.

RED FLAGS

- It's never OK to say, "My customers are not addressing this need today." They are, but it may be by using another, possibly less elegant method. (Before antibiotic cream, for instance, people still tried to remove germs from their cuts and scratches by simply washing with soap and water.)

II

SOLUTION AND BENEFITS

Now that you've used the first three Focal Points to articulate your problem statement, the next two questions give you the opportunity to describe your solution and how customers would benefit.

CHAPTER 4

What Is Your Solution?

Concisely describe your customer solution. What product, service, or product/service combination will you be offering?

You ought to be able to describe your solution in a single sentence. If you're unable to do so, push yourself. Unless and until you can clearly describe your solution in one sentence, you're probably not certain as to what your offering is. Once you've mastered the one-sentence description, it's useful to elaborate with a longer, more detailed description as well.

Eventually, you may find it useful to come up with a series of three product descriptions that progressively track how your product might evolve over time. This "preliminary product road map," depicted in Exhibit B, comprises these three elements:

a. Start by describing your "big vision" for how the product will eventually look—think of it as Version 5.0.
b. Then back off from your big vision to describe the initial launch configuration of the product—Version 1.0, if you will.

c. Finally, describe the minimum viable product, or MVP—that version of the product that you can cobble together as a prelaunch test case that will enable you to gather the most customer input while expending the least effort.

Then, as you further develop your product road map, you can specify in greater levels of detail the intermediate development steps between those three endpoints. Exhibit C provides a sample framework for laying out a more detailed product road map; in this example, we're showing a B2B software product.

Exhibit B

PRELIMINARY PRODUCT ROAD MAP

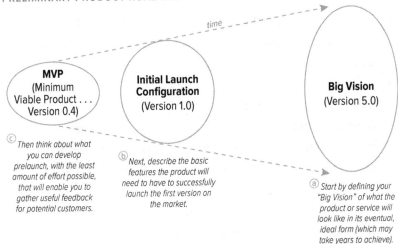

ⓒ Then think about what you can develop prelaunch, with the least amount of effort possible, that will enable you to gather useful feedback for potential customers.

ⓑ Next, describe the basic features the product will need to have to successfully launch the first version on the market.

ⓐ Start by defining your "Big Vision" of what the product or service will look like in its eventual, ideal form (which may take years to achieve).

Exhibit C

FRAMEWORK FOR MORE DETAILED PRODUCT ROAD MAP

(Example for a B2B app for warehouse supervisors and managers)

	MVP	V 1.0	V 2.0	V 5.0
Platform	Wireframe mock-ups	Mobile-friendly web app	Add iOS	Add Android
Language	English	English	Add Spanish	Add Mandarin, Korean, Japanese, French, and German
Vertical markets	NA	Retail distribution centers	Add all warehousing and transportation	Add discrete manufacturing
Application features . . .				
etc. . . .				

TIPS

- Make sure your product descriptions are crisp, clear, and concise. Each one ought to be a strong, stand-alone summary description of your offering.
- Once you've written a draft product description, run it by a few smart people and see if it's perfectly clear to them.
- Start with the big vision / Version 5.0 ideal description of the product. Once you've mastered that, back off from that and think about the subset of features and functions that would be sufficient for your Version 1.0 initial launch configuration. Then you can work on envisioning the MVP—the minimum representation of the product that would suffice as a test case to gather preliminary customer input.
- Don't get too elaborate with your Version 1.0. Keep it simple and try to offer a few elemental features that your target customers will find beneficial. If you try to boil the ocean and make the perfect product before your initial launch, your solution may never see the light of day.

RED FLAGS

- If different people read your product descriptions and come away with different understandings, your description might be ambiguous. Revise it until every reader gets exactly the same takeaway.

CHAPTER 5

How Will Your Customers Benefit?

What is your "value proposition"? Can you quantify that value proposition? That is, how will your customers benefit by switching from the way they're currently addressing their problem to addressing it using your solution?

If customers adopt your solution, explain exactly how they will be able to address their unmet need significantly better, faster, cheaper, and/or cooler than they were formerly able to do so. Be as specific as possible. If you can provide quantitative, as opposed to just qualitative, answers, that's always better.

And remember what we discussed in Focal Point #2 (What is your customers' unmet need?): you'll generally find that you have greater customer demand for a new product that addresses a burning need. So ask yourself, would your solution be solving a "shark-bite pain" (gotta have it) or more of a "mosquito-bite pain" (nice to have it)?

Can you quantify the incremental dollars saved or time saved by customers when using your product? Or, alternatively, the incremental dollars generated? With many consumer products, of course, your value proposition will be primarily *qualitative*, such as the feel-good quotient that a customer gets from wearing a stylish garment or dining at an exquisite restaurant.

Let's look at a few examples of value propositions.

For instance, let's say you're launching an online service that helps high schoolers track their progress toward meeting admission requirements for various colleges. In this case, it's important to understand the compelling value proposition for different groups of customers or constituencies. For high school students, it helps them understand and navigate the college admissions process. For parents, it's important as an aid for their kids to gain acceptance to the best and most appropriate schools possible. For high school guidance counselors, it's a tool for creating a better-informed cohort of advisees and providing them with a more effective college admissions service. And finally, for the colleges themselves, the service results in a better-informed pool of applicants.

Now let's say you're launching a farm-to-table restaurant and market. Once again, it's important to look at the benefits to various constituencies. For diners, they can look forward to enjoying delicious meals with the knowledge that the ingredients are all locally produced—thereby supporting local farmers and generating a smaller carbon footprint. For local farmers, you're providing them with potentially two outlets for their goods—a restaurant and a consumer market—and perhaps brand recognition as well.

How about if your company delivers a cloud-based supply-chain tool that enables global businesses to figure out optimal shipping times, costs, and tariffs. In a B2B case such as this, it's important to try to quantify the benefits. By using this tool, will your business customers do the following?

a. Save time in planning shipments (By how much? What are the time savings and the dollar savings due to greater staff efficiency?)

b. Shorten delivery times (Will this shorten time-to-market and thereby generate an uptick in sales revenue? By how much? Will this shorten delivery times for factory supplies, enabling lowered inventory costs and/or increased production? By how much?)

c. Lower overall tariff expenses (By how much?)

TIPS

- The value proposition for your product may vary for different types of customers or for different constituencies. Be sure you are able to articulate the unique value proposition for each category.
- For B2B products, providing a credible, documented quantification of customer benefits can accelerate the sales process and help justify a higher price.

RED FLAGS

- When articulating your value proposition, stick to the facts. Avoid hyperbole, and don't overstate the benefits.

III

THE MARKET

Now that you've described your customers, the problem you're addressing, and your product and its benefits, it's time to look at the size, nature, and competitiveness of your market.

CHAPTER 6

How Big Is Your Market?

When figuring out your market size, it's useful to estimate a cascading set of three related numbers, as follows:

- **TAM (total addressable market)**—If everyone who could theoretically benefit from your product or service were to do so at the asking price, how big a market would that be, expressed in dollars (or your local currency)?
- **SAM (serviceable addressable market)**—Take the TAM and narrow it down to customers who would realistically use your product and whom you could realistically reach.
- **SOM (serviceable obtainable market)**—From the SAM, further narrow down to reflect your initial target segmentation, initial launch geography, competitive dynamics, production constraints, and so on.

Each level of market estimate should be expressed as an annual revenue number (dollars per year). Your logic in coming up with each estimate is likely to be based on an approximation of the number of customers, multiplied by revenue per customer.

Let's look at a couple illustrative examples.

Introducing the Amazon Kindle in 2007—Estimating the Market

When Amazon was planning to launch its first Kindle e-reader (introduced in 2007), what would their TAM, SAM, and SOM numbers have been? Let's take a crack at coming up with our own back-of-the-envelope estimates (limiting our market numbers to the US for simplicity's sake):

- **TAM for the original Kindle**—Start by coming up with an estimate of all potential users. The US population at the time was 300 million, of which we probably want to include just the literate population (roughly 86 percent), which gives us 258 million people; further narrowing it to those who are between the ages of 15 and 64 (approximately 66 percent), for the sake of discussion, leads us to an estimate of 170 million total potential (US) users. From that start, we want to estimate revenue. We plan to launch the product at a $399 list price and sell e-books for $10 each. (This is how Amazon actually priced in 2007.) If we estimate that of our potential 170 million users, one-third purchase a reader each year (roughly 57 million—notice I'm rounding to avoid false precision) and one-third also purchase one e-book per month (twelve e-books, or $120 per year), that gives us the following calculation:

    (57 million customers per year) × ([$399 for Kindle] + [$120 for e-books]) = <u>a TAM of $30 billion in annual revenue</u> (again, rounding to avoid false precision).

- **SAM for the original Kindle**—Starting with our TAM estimate of $30 billion per year, we now want to narrow it down to those who would realistically use our product and whom we could realistically reach. First, we find a statistic showing that 72 percent of adult Americans read a book in the past year and another stat saying 70 percent of the population is online (in 2007). If we assume, conservatively, that there's no correlation between these two numbers (i.e., that being a book reader does not make one more likely to be online, or vice versa), then we can use the following calculation to estimate SAM:

($30 billion annual TAM) × (72 percent of those who read books) × (70 percent of those who are online) = a SAM of $15 billion per year (rounding).

- **SOM for the original Kindle**—From a TAM of $30 billion per year and a SAM of $15 billion per year, now let's further narrow our estimate to the SOM, or how much of that market we realistically feel we can obtain. Since we're selling both the Kindle e-readers and the associated e-books online, geography is not a constraint (although we're already limiting our estimates, for discussion purposes, to the US). However, because we plan to sell exclusively through the Amazon store, we might need to reduce the number based on the size of the Amazon customer base. At the time, Amazon boasted 76 million user accounts, of which we estimate half, or 38 million, were US customers. That's 22 percent of the 170 million online, book-reading Americans we earlier estimated. Therefore, if we take 22 percent of our SAM, we arrive at the following calculation:

($15 billion annual SAM) × (22 percent) = a SOM of $3.3 billion per year.

(For the sake of this example, we'll just estimate the SOM for a single year rather than, say, for a five-year forecast.)

What might this exercise have told us as Amazon's internal planning team? That the (at the time, nascent) market for e-readers and associated content is sufficiently big to be attractive and a source of incremental growth for us. (Conversely, had we estimated a SOM one-twentieth as large, or $165 million per year, that might well have scared us away from making the necessary investments and taking the associated risks.)

Planning a New Line of Gardening Tools—Estimating the Market

Now let's imagine that you're contemplating launching a new line of high-end gardening hand tools for gardening enthusiasts. Your initial product will be a matched-set trio of a weed-puller, trowel, and hand rake, sold in a $99.99 bundle direct to consumers through your online store. How would you go about estimating your TAM, SAM, and SOM? (Once again, for the sake of simplifying the example, we're going to limit our market numbers to the US.)

- **TAM for our line of gardening hand tools**—We start by estimating the number of home gardeners in the US. A quick search reveals that approximately 118 million people did home gardening in the US within the past twelve months.[*] If everyone who could potentially benefit from our gardening tool offering were to do so at the asking price (rounding to $100 per bundle), that would amount to (118 million customers × $100) $11.8 billion. Of course, that's not an annual revenue number, since this would be a one-time purchase. If we postulate that customers, on average, would purchase an updated tool set every five years, then we can take one-fifth of this number and arrive at <u>an annual TAM of $2.4 billion</u> (rounding).
- **SAM for our line of gardening hand tools**—Starting with our TAM estimate of $2.3 billion per year, we now want to narrow it down to those who would realistically use our product and whom

---

[*] "Number of People Who Did Gardening within the Last 12 Months in the United States from Spring 2008 to Spring 2017 (in Millions)," *Statista*, last modified September 2017, https://www.statista.com/statistics/227419/number-of-gardeners-usa/.

we could realistically reach. We decide that, for a premium-priced product such as ours, we will be targeting those with household incomes of $75,000 or more, which a quick search tells us is approximately 36 percent of US households. And if we choose to pursue only online sales, it makes sense to further narrow the market by two-thirds, surmising that many people would prefer to purchase their gardening tools at a brick-and-mortar store rather than online. These assumptions lead us to the following calculation to estimate the SAM:

($2.3 billion annual TAM) × (36 percent with a household income of $75,000 or more) × (33 percent comfortable purchasing tools online) = a SAM of $275 million per year (rounding—this implies selling 2.75 million units each year at $100 each).

- **SOM for our line of gardening hand tools**—From a TAM of $2.4 billion per year and a SAM of $275 million per year, now let's further narrow our estimate to the SOM, or how much of that market we realistically feel we can obtain. In a case like this with a boutique physical product, the SOM is often limited by production or capital constraints. Let's say that, while our SAM estimate is for 2.75 million unit sales per year, a combination of working capital constraints (i.e., how much money we can afford to tie up in unsold inventory) and production constraints (let's say we're limited in the amount of premium hardwood that's available for the tools' handles) limits us so we can only afford to produce one-fiftieth of that amount. That would result in a SOM calculation of

(55,000 units per year) × ($100 per unit) = a SOM of $5.5 million per year.

This might not be interesting for a large industrial or retail company, but it might prove quite interesting to an entrepreneur contemplating a lifestyle business.

TIPS

- You may want to limit your market estimates to your home country (e.g., just the US or just India) unless you foresee your business expanding beyond those boundaries in the first five years of operation.
- Show your work (document your assumptions).
- Quick order-of-magnitude estimates are fine at the outset.
- Estimate your SOM (serviceable obtainable market, or what you actually hope to achieve) each year for the next five years.
- Be realistic with your SOM estimates.
- For small, local retail businesses, estimating the TAM, SAM, and SOM is less important than for businesses that have national or global aspirations. For instance, if you're starting a hot dog stand, you simply want to ensure that the local foot traffic on your corner is more than adequate during lunch hour to sell out your inventory and nicely exceed breakeven. If you're launching a local exercise studio, your concern is simply that the local market has more than enough potential clients to fill your capacity.
- If you're building an online or mobile business that will be free to many or all users, denominate your market estimates in number of users rather than dollars and cents. (Note that you'll still need a strong business model or a way to make money, which we'll discuss in an upcoming chapter.)

RED FLAGS

- Avoid false precision. These are estimates, so if your computation comes to $491.35 million, round that to $490 million; after all, it's likely based on assumptions that are themselves approximations.

- If your SOM estimate is larger than the size of existing, comparable industries or markets, you're probably being too optimistic. For instance, if you're contemplating launching a high-end, specialty bicycle maker, and your SOM estimate is $4 billion per year—or roughly two-thirds of the entire existing US bicycle market—logic would suggest that you're being wildly optimistic.

CHAPTER 7

Which Customer Segments Will You Target, and Why?*

In business-planning parlance, the process of addressing this Focal Point is often referred to as STP, or segmentation, targeting, and positioning. At a high level, you can think of STP this way:

- Segmentation—Breaking down the overall market by identifying groups of customers with similar needs and/or similar responses to a given marketing mix.
- Targeting—Selecting those groups of customers (segments) that you wish to serve.

---

* The material in this chapter is based on overview material on segmentation, targeting, and positioning described in class slides originally developed by Professor Eugene W. Anderson, PhD. The author has expanded on Anderson's material and adapted it to the realm of entrepreneurship.

- Positioning—Articulating "points of difference" that will make your product or service competitive in your target segment.

By going through this process, you'll be able to determine (a) who is (and who is not) a customer, (b) who is (and is not) a competitor, and (c) what marketing and sales activities are (and are not) important for success. Focus is crucial for startup success, and proper segmentation helps you focus by

- designing a marketing program that effectively reaches your target customers; and
- clearly identifying "value drivers"—that is, what are the things that your target customers truly care about versus what doesn't matter or is less important?

STP helps focus your limited resources and efforts for maximum effect, and it improves your startup's ability to compete by being great at a few things rather than trying to be all things to all people.

Let's take a closer look at each of the STP steps.

Segmentation

First off, take your overall market and think about useful ways to slice or divide it that might provide you with meaningful market subsets or segments. For many markets, an obvious place to start is by dividing the market by geography. For someone who's renting heavy equipment, for instance, is she focusing on a specific county? If another entrepreneur is selling CRM (customer relationship management) software, is he starting out focusing on the US market? Is the owner of a newly opened bar focusing primarily on residents for whom the location is within walking distance of home or work?

In addition, you may slice the market in other ways that are useful. For instance, our bar owner may be targeting customers not only geographically (those within walking distance) but also demographically (e.g., college educated, with a certain level of household income), behaviorally (say, social-media savvy), as well as psychographically (hipster millennials, for instance).

These different ways to slice the market for the purpose of defining segments are sometimes referred to as "descriptors." Exhibits D and E provide examples of segment descriptors for business-to-consumer (B2C) and business-to-business (B2B) markets, respectively.

How can you tell whether you've identified useful or meaningful segments? For each identified segment, use these four screening questions:

1. **Is it substantial?** Will the size and growth of the segment justify a separate marketing mix?
2. **Is it accessible?** Can the segment be reached and served efficiently?
3. **Is it identifiable?** Can you reliably determine who is a member of this segment?
4. **Is there a differential response?** Do members of this segment respond in a distinctive way to a given marketing mix?

EXHIBIT D

B2C MARKETS—EXAMPLES OF SEGMENT DESCRIPTORS

Geographic	Demographic	Behavioral	Psychographic
Hemisphere	Age	Media behavior	Lifestyle
Continent	Gender	Solutions or substitutes used	Values
Country	Household income	Complements used	Goals
Region	Education	Usage patterns	Motivation
State	Occupation	Shopping behavior	Personality
County or metro area	Ethnicity and language		Aspirations
Neighborhood	Religion		Attitudes

EXHIBIT E

B2B MARKETS—EXAMPLES OF SEGMENT DESCRIPTORS

Geographic	Demographic	Behavioral	Organizational
Hemisphere	Industry (line of business)	Urgency	Risk profile
Continent	Organization type	Type of application or use	Decision-making unit
Country	Organization size	Order size	Buyer similarity
Region	Type of technology	Order frequency	Buyer perceptions
State	End-user type		Purchase process
County or metro area	End use		Purchase criteria
Neighborhood			

So to return to our bar owner, is her chosen segment that we laid out earlier (social media–savvy, college-grad, millennial hipsters with a certain household income, for whom the bar is within walking distance of work or home) (a) substantial (lots of people who'd be likely to fill the place night after night), (b) accessible (can she reach them efficiently and effectively—for example, through their chosen social media channels?), (c) identifiable (is it clear who's in and out of this segment?), and (d) one that will respond in a clearly distinguishable way to a marketing mix (e.g., they tend to belong to one or a few self-referencing groups that already connect, talk, and compare notes—for instance, using specific apps and social media tools to decide where to meet up and hang out after work)?

Targeting

Once you have identified viable segments, the next challenge is to evaluate the relative appeal or attractiveness of each, with the purpose of selecting segments to target. Exhibit F provides a framework

Exhibit F

SEGMENT ATTRACTIVENESS FACTORS

Customers	Competition	Company
Size and growth	Positions	Fit with goals
Acquisition and retention	Capabilities	
Network effects	Anticipated rivalry	
Bargaining power	Substitutes and new entrants	

Exhibit G

IDENTIFYING THE IDEAL TARGET SEGMENTS

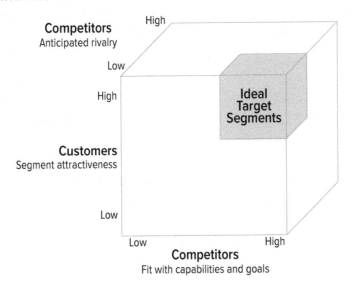

highlighting the key factors to consider when evaluating the relative attractiveness of one segment versus another.

How do we apply these factors to decide which segments are more attractive than others? As we illustrate in Exhibit G, all other things being equal, the most appealing segments are those that

- rank high on the customer scale (substantial, accessible, identifiable, and different),

- rank low in terms of anticipated rivalry from competitors (clearly differentiated and have an unmet market need), and
- are a good fit with the company's core competencies and goals.

Positioning

Once you've completed your segmentation and targeting, ask yourself how to clearly position your product or service offering for each target segment. You began addressing the positioning task in Focal Point #5 (How will your customers benefit?). Another excellent positioning tool is the perceptual map, described in Focal Point #8 (Who are your competitors, and how do you compare?), which follows.

Ultimately, it's useful to distill your positioning for each target segment down to a simple positioning statement, as follows:

"_____ (*identify the product*) is the
_____ (*identify the category*) that
_____ (*describe the key points of dif-*
ference and primary benefits)."

Using our previous bar-owner example, that positioning statement might go something like this for our bar owner:

"*Megan's Place is the perfect watering hole where millennials can connect with friends in the evening over single-cask bourbons and artisanal, farm-to-table bar food.*"

TIPS

- As you develop and prioritize your segments, think of it as a process of setting up bowling pins: the front bowling pin is the ideal one to hit first, and if you hit it properly, it'll help you knock down other bowling pins (subsequent target segments). So what does that suggest about selecting your front bowling pin? It doesn't have to be the biggest, but it ought to be easy to knock down—classic early adopters, interested in trying something new, and the type of customers who will be influential to later adopters.

 RED FLAGS

- If you define a segment that you can't figure out how to reach with a focused marketing campaign and/or one in which the customers don't share the same needs and wants regarding your product, that suggests it's not a well-defined and useful market segment.

CHAPTER 8

Who Are Your Competitors, and How Do You Compare?

Describe your competitive positioning and your competitive differentiation. And remember, even if you're introducing a solution that you consider an industry first, you will be asking your customers to change the way they're currently doing things. So even if you think you have a novel solution, you *do* indeed have competition—namely, the way your target customers are currently addressing their need.

For example, you may be opening your new coffee shop in a neighborhood with no direct competition, but you do have competition: your target customers are currently brewing coffee at home or perhaps waiting for their caffeine fix until they get into work.

Similarly, the first-generation iPod (launched in 2001) and other early MP3 players may have had very little direct competition in terms of MP3 digital music players then on the market. But they were going up against the entrenched competition of CDs (iPod's competitive advantages being its smaller format and greater storage capacity) and the radio (iPod's advantage being users' ability to determine their own playlists).

One commonly used format for summarizing your competitive positioning is the competitive positioning matrix shown in Exhibit H.

The competitive positioning matrix can be used to simply indicate "Yes" or "No" for each feature. Alternatively, you may wish to show a greater level of granularity by indicating each competitor's degree of coverage on each feature with a score, say from one (low) to three (high), and then tallying a total for each competitor. A similar approach is to use stoplight color codes for each cell (red for poor, yellow for middling, and green for strong).

Another useful framework for describing how your startup or brand fits relative to competitors is the perceptual map. Using this approach, you select two axes that are particularly relevant to your market and then array your company and your competitors along both those axes.

Exhibits I and J offer some illustrative examples.

EXHIBIT H

TYPICAL COMPETITIVE POSITIONING MATRIX

Key Product Features or Beneficial Characteristics	Your Product	Competitor A	Competitor B	Competitor C	Competitor D
Feature 1	X		X		
Feature 2	X	X			X
Feature 3		X		X	
Feature 4	X		X		
Feature 5	X			X	X

Exhibit I

PERCEPTUAL MAP—EXAMPLE FOR CARS

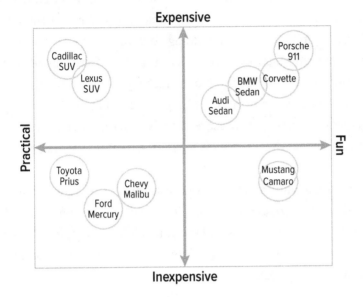

Exhibit J

PERCEPTUAL MAP—EXAMPLE FOR FAST FOOD RESTAURANTS

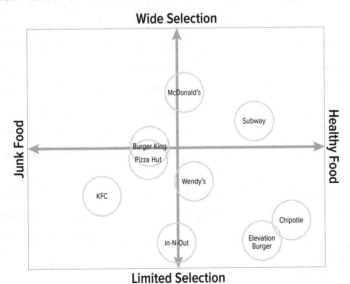

TIPS

- Cautionary note: If you do an online search for your concept and find that there are other companies—either startups or larger companies—already doing something similar, the natural human reaction is to be discouraged ("Darn, my idea is already taken!"). But think of it this way: if others are already pursuing this idea (or something close), that could be seen as *market validation*. If there is truly a market need for your solution, then you can view current activity in the market as confirmation that yours is not a crazy idea.

- Be realistic and honest in your assessments of your product and those of your competitors. It's often useful to put yourself in the customers' shoes and ask yourself how they perceive all the products. If you falsely inflate your competitive advantage, you're only hurting yourself.

RED FLAGS

- If your product or service is equivalent to, or only marginally better than, well-established competitors, you might want to think twice about launching the business. To have a sustainable competitive advantage and build market share, you will need to offer your target customers a solution that is *dramatically* better/faster/cheaper/cooler than their current alternatives.

- Not all features or characteristics are equally important in the eyes of your customers. In your competitive positioning table, think about listing the features or characteristics in approximate order of weight or importance. And be mindful that if your column has the most boxes checked but you're missing the most important one or two, you may still struggle to compete.

IV

BUSINESS MODEL

These next four Focal Points will help you better understand your business model. You'll start by describing your revenue model (how you'll make money). But in defining your business model, it's important not to stop there. You should explain the planned pricing of your product or service. It's also important to capture a preliminary sense of what business functions you'll perform in-house versus outsource.

CHAPTER 9

How Will Your Business Make Money?

In business parlance, what is your revenue model (the narrowest definition of your business model)? Let's look at some examples.

Let's say your new business would be providing power tools and equipment (e.g., power washers, carpet cleaners, paint sprayers, etc.). Is your plan to generate revenue by purchasing these tools at wholesale and then selling them at a retail markup? Alternatively, do you plan on owning the equipment and renting it out by the day or by the hour? Or are you thinking of providing a turnkey service in which customers can arrange to pay by the hour for a skilled operator to come on-site with the equipment to perform a job? Or is your plan to generate revenue using some combination of these approaches?

What if you're opening a guitar shop? Is your plan to sell new guitars? Buy, fix up, and resell used guitars? Sell other people's used guitars on consignment (where the original owner retains ownership and you provide a sales venue and collect a commission if it sells)? Are you planning to rent guitars, amps, and other equipment to consumers? Offer repair services? Music lessons? Some combination of these?

If you're contemplating a doggy-daycare business, what might your revenue model be? Do you charge by the day or by the month for daycare for working dog owners? Do you offer multiday, 24/7 lodging (luxury kennel) services when dog owners are out of town? While my pet is staying at your daycare place, can I arrange for add-on services such as grooming or training? Do you charge me on a per-case basis, and/or can I purchase a subscription for periodic grooming or training? Are you charging differentially for different types of food or nutritional supplements—or for toys, leashes, and paraphernalia?

As these examples illustrate, a company may have multiple revenue models that complement one another. For instance, a golf-oriented website may make money through a combination of (a) Google AdWords advertising, (b) display advertising, (c) affiliate marketing (selling books, videos, and golf wear on their site through Amazon and other retailers and receiving affiliate sales commissions), and (d) sales commissions for teaching referrals to golf pros. And in such an instance where a company has complementary revenue models, there's no requirement that they all have to be implemented concurrently; in other words, the entrepreneurs may consider "turning them on" one at a time as they make sense and as the managers have the time and resources.

 TIPS

- Depending on your business, it's often appropriate to have multiple, complementary revenue models. List all that may apply, in order of importance or primacy (i.e., which ones will actually drive the business vs. be ancillary revenue sources).
- If you anticipate having multiple revenue sources, also think about the sequence in which each source is likely to kick in as

you grow the business. For instance, for an online business or mobile app, do you need to grow your user base to a certain minimum size before you can sell advertising? Or perhaps you anticipate generating revenue through data analytics (aggregating and analyzing customer data), which may also require first building up a certain critical mass of users and usage history.

 RED FLAGS

- "Building up our user base and then selling out to Alphabet, Amazon, or Facebook" is not a revenue model; it's an exit strategy. It's important to have a clear plan as to how your business will actually make money.

CHAPTER 10

How Will You Price Your Product?

How much are you charging, for what type of transaction, and to whom?

Do you charge one time up front plus an annual maintenance contract? Or will you charge a monthly or annual subscription fee? (If it's a subscription fee, do you charge prospectively for each use period, or retrospectively?) A common pricing model for many online and mobile businesses, for instance, is the so-called freemium model, wherein the basic app or service is free to all, with an optional premium version available for a subscription fee.

Service businesses, ranging from electricians to certified public accountants, often set a minimum fee for a customer engagement, and then charge a certain amount per person-hour above a certain level; lawyers and consultants may charge a standard hourly rate and then require an up-front retainer that prepays for twenty or more hours.

TIPS

- In determining your pricing, consider the "price umbrella" in the market (i.e., how much others charge for competitive or comparable products). The ambient pricing of comparable products will help you determine what the market is already accustomed to seeing in terms of both level of price as well as structure (i.e., one-time payment vs. annual subscription, or hourly fees for a service vs. pricing by the job).

- Also consider economic value added (EVA) pricing, especially effective in B2B businesses. Using the EVA approach, you try to quantify and document the economic benefit that accrues to the customer from using your product or service, and then set your pricing to charge a reasonable fraction of that EVA (perhaps 10–15 percent) that's palatable to the customer.

RED FLAGS

- Avoid being the low-priced competitor. A trap many entrepreneurs fall into is what you might think of as "apologetic pricing": *Please consider buying from us. I'm sorry, I know you haven't heard of us before because we're new and unestablished, so we offer our product for less than the established players.* Instead, consider the "proud pricing" approach: *We're launching this business because we firmly believe in our unique value proposition; we look forward to explaining that to customers and charging a premium price for a superior product.* Positioning yourself as the low-price market offering is a competitive strategy that tends to only work for large, undifferentiated retailers and similar businesses, and it is a poor prescription for entrepreneurial startup success. Being the low-priced competitor tends to require massive operational and financial scale and often results in an undifferentiated product or service offering and a business with very narrow profit margins.

CHAPTER 11

Which Functions Will You Perform In-House versus Outsource?

A key aspect of your business model is considering which business functions you plan to perform in-house, with your company's staff, and which functions you plan to outsource. If you're producing a physical product, for example, do you plan to outsource the detailed design to a design consultancy or do all the design work yourselves? Are you planning on building the product yourselves or hiring one or more contract manufacturers for that task? Will you sell through your own e-commerce site, through traditional retail outlets, or both? How about warehousing of inventory? Packaging, shipping, and order fulfillment?

Additionally, do you need to have a full-time accountant or attorney on your team, or are the accounting, bookkeeping, finance, and legal functions activities you can tackle by contracting by the hour with firms or freelancers that do that for a living? How about marketing? Customer service?

Bear in mind that there is no "right answer" to these questions. Often, the answer for a given startup as to which functions are performed in-house is determined by the skills and experience of the core team. You may also wish to outsource most business functions at first to keep your early-stage fixed costs low; then, as the business grows, you can consider bringing various functions in-house as it makes sense from a cost and efficiency perspective.

 TIPS

- Focus on what you do best—your core competencies.
- Don't outsource the magic, or "secret sauce," of your business. If you're building a B2B software business, don't outsource the software development. On the other hand, if you need to develop or customize certain software for your operation, but it's ancillary to your business mission, then it's fine to outsource its development and maintenance.
- Be creative. You may wish to outsource a number of business functions at first—for example, shipping, accounting and bookkeeping, or help-desk services—to keep your fixed operating costs low and minimize the amount of capital that's required to launch your business. Then, as you grow, you can bring these outsourced functions in-house by making permanent hires as they can be subsidized by your larger business base.

 RED FLAGS

- Be careful about outsourcing sales. The first instinct of founders with no sales experience is often to avoid doing the selling activity themselves. They'll often try to find outside marketing agencies and distributors to peddle their products;

alternatively, they'll say that a salesperson will be their first internal hire. Remember, though, that in the vast majority of startups, nobody is more effective at representing the company's products or services to customers—and closing those first few crucial sales—than the founders. Furthermore, selling through distributors or resellers can be problematic, since such third parties are never as motivated as the startup itself to land customers, especially in the early stages.

CHAPTER 12

How Scalable Is Your Business?

All other things being equal, businesses that are easy and inexpensive to scale are more appealing than those that are not. The concept of scalability is frequently equated to capital efficiency; that is, can you grow a company—from small-scale to large-scale—by injecting only a modest amount of investment money (capital)?

Two companies may be in the same business sector or industry yet have business models that make them more or less scalable, respectively. Let's take the example of two entrepreneurs who are both passionate about the growing market for organic, grass-fed beef.

- Entrepreneur A takes the approach of buying a ranch, breeding grass-fed, organic cattle, and selling the beef from his small herd of cows to consumers and restaurants (in purchase lots of hundreds of pounds each). This business model is very capital inefficient and not easy to scale. It's quite expensive to launch (lots of money is required to buy the land, the equipment, the livestock, the feed, and so on) and also very slow, difficult, and expensive to scale (scaling requires either breeding and raising or acquiring additional livestock, and the size of the operation is ultimately limited by the grazing acreage).

- Entrepreneur B builds an online, two-sided network that serves as a marketplace connecting sellers of organic, grass-fed beef (mostly small ranchers/farmers) with consumers and restaurants who wish to purchase that beef. Unlike Entrepreneur A's business, her approach is very capital efficient and highly scalable. It costs far less money and time to establish—just building an internet platform and recruiting sellers and buyers. It's also dramatically easier and less expensive to scale—no capital tied up in inventory, each new transaction has an incremental "production cost" of zero, and the business charges a highly profitable transaction fee.

Now let's look at a professional services example, in which two entrepreneurs both possess deep expertise in helping high schoolers identify and gain acceptance to the right colleges.

- Entrepreneur C sets up his own consulting firm and sells his advisory services to parents to coach them and their kids on navigating the college selection and entrance process. Because of his reputation and expertise, he's able to charge a lucrative hourly rate, and positive word of mouth enables him to successfully grow his customer base. However, this business model is very difficult to scale, since it's difficult to grow the client base beyond the number of clients the founder can advise himself; it's challenging to find fellow counselors with his level of expertise. Furthermore, natural client turnover—once a child leaves for college, his services are no longer required—means he's constantly hustling to find new clients.

- Entrepreneur D takes a different approach and establishes an internet platform for college entrance counseling. She provides some information for free and charges subscription fees for premium content (i.e., evaluation tests to help focus an individual's search or video-coaching sessions on various topics). Her site also includes a platform for connecting expert college counselors from around the country with teens; the site charges a fee for the one-on-one sessions, pays the counselor, and collects a transaction fee. You can see how this business model is dramatically more scalable than the other. Unlike Entrepreneur C's approach, the capacity of Entrepreneur D's business to expand is not constrained by her time and availability, and as the base of content subscribers and online counseling users grows, she doesn't have to add significant costs (e.g., expensive expert coaches) to enable that growth.

None of these four business-model examples is wrong. At the end of the day, all entrepreneurs should build businesses that work well for them and make them happy. However, you can see how Entrepreneurs B and D in these examples, by building highly scalable businesses, have greater potential to achieve an appealing dream: at some point, they'll wake up and realize their business was earning money for them while they slept.

TIPS

- Explore different approaches, or business models, for serving your market. It often helps to look at examples in comparable or adjacent markets. (i.e., if you're looking at establishing a tea business, look at the various approaches that have been working in coffee.)
- As you examine different business constructs for your market, ask yourself these key questions: How much would it cost to

set up this business? How much (in money and time) would it cost to scale or grow it?

- Bear in mind that you can start with one business model and evolve to something more scalable over time. For instance, you may begin with charging by the hour for consulting services to generate initial revenue and learn your customers' needs, then use that revenue to fund the development of packaged solutions—books, online tools, and software—that can be developed once but sold many times.

 RED FLAGS

- Personal services businesses—ranging from consulting, to accounting and bookkeeping, to personal training, to building trades such as plumbing, electrical, or carpentry—are difficult to scale, because scaling the business requires you to hire, train, and retain additional service professionals with the appropriate skills.
- Businesses that require significant up-front investment capital to achieve growth are very challenging to scale. For instance, if you launch a restaurant or store, even if it's very successful, expanding to multiple physical stores—creating a chain under the same brand—could cost hundreds of thousands of dollars in investment capital for each new location. An alternative to scaling such an operation is to explore the franchise business model, in which you license your brand and formulaic approach to your restaurant or store to other entrepreneurs, known as franchisees, who then use their own capital to build each new location and pay you franchise fees.

V

MARKETING AND SALES

By addressing the next three questions, you will develop a good preliminary understanding of your approach to marketing and sales.

CHAPTER 13

How Will You Gather Customer Input?

What is your customer involvement strategy? Note that I'm posing this as a rhetorical question: well-run startups all incorporate input from customers, and the very best really bring lead customers into the creative process of specifying, critiquing, modifying, and improving the company's product offerings from the very beginning.

The process of gathering customer input during the initial planning process is often referred to as customer discovery, but you might think of it as *community discovery*. In community discovery, you want to seek out the different "classes of customers"—for example, potential end users as well as economic buyers (purchasing decision makers, if they're different from the end users) and influencers. If you have a health care app, for instance, you may want to talk not only to patients (potential end users) but also to insurance companies (perhaps the economic buyers) and clinicians (influencers and perhaps data consumers). If you're imagining an after-school coding clinic for kids, then it would be wise to talk not only to children in your target age range (potential end users) but also to parents (the economic buyers), teachers, and school administrators (influencers and possibly business partners whose facilities could host your classes). Meanwhile, if you're contemplating a retail product—let's say a niche food product—it's important to gather input not only from consumers but from potential retail outlets as well.

Ask open-ended questions. You might start with some variation of Focal Points #2 and #3 of the Launch Lens: What is your unmet need? And how are you addressing this need today? Then explore current challenges: Do you view the way you're addressing things today as an effective approach? If not, what would you like to see changed or improved—what characteristics would you like to see in a more effective approach? If a better solution to your need were available, what would it take (in terms of features, convenience, price, etc.) to cause you to switch from your current approach?

Community discovery is often best conducted through face-to-face (or live phone or online) conversations; both one-on-one and focus group discussions can be effective. As you develop a clearer picture of customer needs through face-to-face interviews, this kind of input can be supplemented by custom surveys targeting a broader, national (or international) audience. Some online survey services offer to conduct your survey with an audience customized to your needs (e.g., parents of middle school–aged kids on the Atlantic seaboard or type 1 diabetes patients in the US) at a modest extra cost.

Then as you develop a minimum viable product (MVP) to demonstrate proof of concept for your solution, continue to use your different classes of customers as sounding boards. When you're close to commercial release of a product or service, conduct beta testing (typically a controlled, two- to six-month trial by a handful of customers who promise to provide constructive feedback).

In addition to all these approaches, many startups find splash pages (a.k.a. launch pages) to be a very effective way to gauge early interest in their product; these can be used for online or mobile offerings as well as physical products. A launch page is used to preannounce a product and provide a simple way for customers to register on an opt-in email list for notification when the product is launched— thus giving the startup a way to measure customer demand and build a contact list of prequalified sales prospects.

Exhibit K summarizes the various approaches to gathering customer input.

EXHIBIT K

METHODS OF GATHERING CUSTOMER INPUT

Method of Gathering Customer Input	Description
Community discovery	One-on-one interviews with end users, economic buyers, influencers, and potential channel partners (e.g., retailers or distributors)
	Focus groups (exploratory discussions with select groups of target customers)
Launch page	A web page used to preannounce a product, gauge interest, and accumulate a prequalified email list of prospective customers
Beta testing	Two- to six-month testing of a prelaunch version of your product, with a controlled group of customers, to seek constructive input and critique prior to commercial launch
Surveys	Online surveys can be used at various stages, from early customer discovery to postlaunch customer input

TIPS

- Make sure you're going into your conversations with prospective customers, partners, and so on with an open mind. Your job is to listen and learn, not to inform and explain.

RED FLAGS

- If you go into conversations believing you already have all the answers, you'll end up trying to explain and convince rather than exploring, listening, and learning.

CHAPTER 14

How Will Your Customers Acquire Your Product?

From the very beginning of the planning process, it's important to think about how your customers will acquire your product (a.k.a. determining your distribution channels).

First, let's look at consumer products (so-called B2C, or business-to-consumer, businesses). Will you be selling it online? If so, will that be through your own online store? An Amazon store? Alternatively, if you're planning to sell through brick-and-mortar stores, which ones? Do you have a sense of whether they'd be interested in carrying your product? If so, under what circumstances? (What are their typical terms and conditions, including wholesale discounts, piloting in a single store, volume and inventory expectations, expectations on vendors for comarketing/promotion, payments for product placement, etc.?) In addition, in some industries (alcoholic beverages, for instance), retail outlets might only purchase through intermediary distributors.

If, on the other hand, you're building a B2B startup, you have a different set of distribution considerations. Are you planning to sell to your customers by generating leads online and fulfilling them through a combination of online sales (customers doing self-service purchasing through your website) and inside sales (employees or contractors fulfilling information requests and completing sales through email, phone, or online chat)? While these modes tend to work well for many B2B products, big-ticket items—those in which individual sales amount to tens or hundreds of thousands of dollars or more—often require field sales (employees visiting customers in person) to complement inside sales.

Like B2C businesses, B2B startups may also wish to consider indirect sales channels (distributors or resellers) as part of the distribution mix. And note that direct sales (either inside or field sales) and indirect sales are not mutually exclusive. You may choose to sell direct to major customer accounts while using resellers for small accounts; you may wish to sell direct in your home country while selling through distributors in foreign markets.

 TIPS

- If you've got a physical consumer product you're planning to sell through traditional, brick-and-mortar retail, it's tough to have a viable business unless you can achieve a production cost (cost of goods sold, or COGS) of approximately one-quarter of your target MSRP (manufacturer's suggested retail price). Retail outlets will typically ask for a wholesale discount of up to 50 percent—more from large chains, less from boutiques. Then, as the manufacturer or vendor, you'll need half of that remaining 50 percent to cover all marketing, overhead, and profit.

- For consumer products, online and brick-and-mortar distribution are not mutually exclusive. Many businesses begin by selling online—to build up a loyal brand following and generate strong profits—and later follow with the addition of brick-and-mortar distribution to build volume.
- For B2B businesses, while inside sales and online sales are very appealing due to their low cost, bigger-ticket items (more expensive products or services) will often require some level of field sales activity, particularly with larger customers.

 RED FLAGS

- If you're considering multiple, complementary distribution channels (e.g., direct-to-consumer online plus brick-and-mortar retail plus private label resale), don't assume that you need to launch them all simultaneously. It's OK, and often helpful, to consider staging your channels one at a time.

CHAPTER 15

How Will You Promote to Your Customers?

By this point, you've already done a good job of describing your customers and the problem they face (Focal Points #1–3), as well as your solution and its compelling value proposition (Focal Points #4 and 5). You've also figured out your target market segments and how you'll ideally position yourself in those segments against competitors (Focal Points #7 and 8). And you've thought about how your customers will buy your product (distribution channels, Focal Point #14).

Based on that conceptual foundation—you know who your customers are, what you're offering, why they should care, and how or where they're going to buy—you're now ready to figure out the best way to promote your product or service. Let's start by examining a tool that will help you organize your thinking, known as the AIDA framework (for Awareness, Interest, Desire, and Action), illustrated in Exhibit L.

In the AIDA framework, your first marketing challenge is to establish awareness among target customers ("suspects")—to inform your universe of target customers that your product or service exists. This is

Exhibit L

THE AIDA FRAMEWORK FOR MARKETING AND SALES

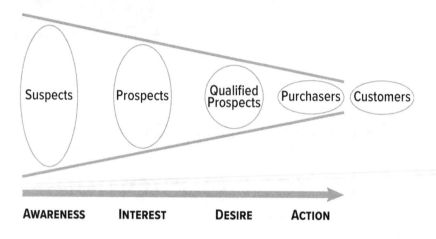

often referred to as promotion, or marketing promotion, and is used to build awareness and brand recognition among your target customers. Then, systematically, your challenge is to winnow the target customer universe of "suspects," who are simply aware, leaving "prospects" with whom you've established interest in your product. From there, you want to further winnow from the list "prospects" with interest, leaving "qualified prospects" with whom you've established desire to purchase your product. And finally, you need to work to motivate your "qualified prospects" to become "purchasers" who take action to buy.

Using this framework, start thinking about what cost-effective marketing mix you can use to systematically establish awareness, interest, desire, and action. The promotional methods you select will depend on the nature of your product or service. Is it B2C or B2B? Can you reach your target customers through tightly self-referencing groups—that is, through existing, trusted networks to which they already belong and through which they already communicate?

Let's look at a B2B example: a cloud-based software offering that helps doctors with patient diagnoses and identifying drug interactions. In this case, examples of tightly self-referencing groups might be national and state medical associations and professional societies, with potential to reach your target customers through their associated newsletters and conferences. The marketing mix in this case could include continuing medical education (CME) courses that incorporate your solution, booth displays and ads at national or state medical society conferences, an opt-in email newsletter, and placement of user success-story articles in professional and trade journals.

A B2C example might be jewelry that features college logos. Here, self-referencing groups might include sororities. The marketing mix in this case could entail trunk shows at sorority houses, campus reps, and providing sororities with fund-raising opportunities by offering to donate a certain percentage of profits to that chapter's favorite charity for all referred sales. In B2C markets in particular, it's useful to identify marketing methods that are self-perpetuating and for which you get "free advertising" through word of mouth (WOM), viral excitement, and customer referrals.

 TIPS

- Paid advertising tends to be very expensive and impractical for a startup. Alternatively, seek to garner so-called earned media, such as press coverage and mentions from key influencers such as bloggers.
- The most effective promotion is positive word of mouth. Find inexpensive, clever ways to get customers to refer their friends and colleagues.
- Take advantage of social media, and choose carefully: Instagram might be great for targeting young consumers, while Twitter and LinkedIn might be more effective for a B2B audience.

 RED FLAGS

- Less is often more. Too many startups fail because they overspend on marketing, working hard (or expensively) rather than working smart.

VI

FINANCE

The next three questions will help you think through some of the key money issues associated with your startup business

CHAPTER 16

How Much Will It Cost to Launch the Business?

It's important to figure out how much money it will take to do everything necessary to prepare the business for launch. Obviously, the lower you can make this number, the easier and less financially risky it will be to get the business off the ground. Exhibit M enumerates some of the typical categories of one-time launch expenses.

Exhibit M

Category of One-Time $ Launch Expense	Comments
Legal	This includes developing the legal paperwork and filing your legal entity (company) with the state and the IRS. It also includes basic contracts with contractors, purchase-and-sale or license agreements with customers, and so on.
Product development	For a physical product, you'll need to develop preliminary prototypes and final designs that are manufacturable. For software or an app, you'll need to allocate cost to design, code, and test.
Operations	Include here any production or manufacturing equipment you'll need (i.e., if you're producing a physical product). For a software or online business, include hosting costs.
Initial marketing expenses	Basic branding often includes developing a company/product name, logo, and tagline. Initial market expenses may include website development and both online and offline promotion.

(continued)

Category of One-Time Launch Expense	$	Comments
Materials and product inventory		For a physical product, do you need to purchase or produce a minimum quantity of product to have in your inventory before you launch the business? (For a software business, an app, and so on, you'll have no cost here.)
Leases and leasehold improvements		For a store or restaurant, signing a long-term lease and paying for the leasehold improvements for the new space can be significant. Warehouse space should also be included here. On the other hand, for an online or mobile business, you'll typically have no expense here.
Baseline salaries and benefits		Include here salaries or contractor fees for any employees necessary to get the business launched. If it's possible for the founders to "launch this on the side" without quitting their day jobs, not including founders' salaries will keep overall launch costs down.
Others?		
TOTAL		

TIPS

- If it's possible to launch your business "on the side" without quitting your day job, then don't include founders' salaries in this calculation.

RED FLAGS

- In calculating your launch costs, focus only on what it will take to get the business set up and "open for business." Do not include expenses you're going to incur on an ongoing or recurring basis once the business is up and running.
- Avoid false precision. The purpose of this exercise is to approximate the amount of money you'll need to launch. Therefore, it's probably useful to round to the nearest $1,000.

CHAPTER 17

Can the Business Generate Sustainably High Profits?

Think of profit as revenue minus expenses—that is, as the money left over in the business after all expenses are paid. Expenses include the cost of producing and shipping the product (the so-called cost of goods sold); service costs directly related to a sale; and so-called overhead costs, including salaries, facility rent, utilities, software hosting, and other ongoing costs. Are you able to make a profit on each unit sold or with each new customer engagement? Are you able to turn a profit on a month-to-month or quarter-to-quarter basis? Exhibit N explains how to calculate profit.

Once you've figured out your profit numbers in dollars and cents, you can easily calculate your profitability ratios (profit as a percentage of revenue), which are even more informative.

Exhibit N

SIMPLE PROFIT CALCULATION

		Comments/Explanations
Revenue	$_____	Include all sources of incoming revenue (a.k.a. sales)
– Variable costs	($_____)	Expenses that you only incur when you sell or produce incremental units or garner new customers, a.k.a. "cost of goods sold" (COGS)
= Gross profit	$_____	
– Overhead + fixed costs	($_____)	Expenses you're incurring regardless of the number of sales or customers. Include facility rent, equipment, and salaries
= Operating profit	$_____	Profit before taxes (accountants may refer to it as EBITDA, or "earnings before interest, taxes, depreciation, and amortization")

- Gross profit margin (a.k.a. gross margin) = (gross profit for a given period) / (revenue for that same period)

    Expressed as a percentage, this ratio tells you how profitable you are on a per-unit, customer-by-customer basis.

- Operating profit margin (a.k.a. operating margin) = (operating profit for a given period) / (revenue for that same period)

    As with gross margin, operating margin is expressed as a percentage, or profit as a proportion of revenue (sales). This is a strong measure of overall cash profitability of the business.

Why is strong, consistent profitability important for a business? To put it simply, if your business is not consistently profitable, it won't be sustainable. And be aware that different industries or market sectors have different profitability norms. Restaurants, for example, are known for running on very thin operating margins for food service but finding alcohol sales to be very profitable. In general, sales of undifferentiated products or services—commodities ranging from groceries to steel to moving services—will have narrow profit margins. Online and software companies, by contrast, tend to operate at very high profit margins due to the fact that delivering the solution to each incremental customer doesn't cost the business much at all.

 TIPS

- When doing your profit calculations, it's useful to calculate revenue as sales net of distribution costs. For instance, if you're selling a consumer product through retail outlets, whereas your MSRP may be $100, it's likely that you'll be selling to your retail channel for a wholesale price that might be only half of that, or $50; in that example, use the wholesale revenue ($50 per unit) as the revenue assumption in your profit calculation.

 RED FLAGS

- Avoid false precision; since these are estimates, it's OK to round your numbers.
- A common entrepreneur's mistake is to expect your startup to be magically more profitable than other companies already operating in your industry. Through your network or searching online, inquire about the typical profit ratios for your type of business, and those will give you a reality check as to whether your estimates are too optimistic.

CHAPTER 18

At What Point Could You Quit Your Day Job?

These days, it's not uncommon for entrepreneurs to launch their new business in a "side-hustle" mode; they mitigate the financial risk by keeping their day job and focusing on their startup during evenings and weekends. But before jumping in, even on a side-hustle basis, do yourself a favor and do a quick calculation to answer the question "When could you quit your day job (i.e., at what point would your startup be able to support you with a paycheck and benefits)?"

To figure this out, use a simple tool called a reverse income statement. (Don't worry; it's easier than it sounds.) Here's how it works, step-by-step:

- Decide on your base salary requirements.
- Figure out the cost of benefits (safe bet: 25 percent of base salary).

- Define your overhead expenses for the baseline business.
  - office rent and utilities (or can you operate this out of a spare bedroom?)
  - purchase of computers and office equipment
  - marketing expenses
  - administrative expenses
- How much does that add up to per month? That number equals your Total Monthly Expenses, or the minimum level of expenses you need to cover each month, were you to quit your day job and devote all your efforts to your startup.
- In Focal Point #17, you figured out your gross profit per unit sold.
- Given your gross profit per unit, how many units do you need to sell in order to break even each month or cover your monthly expenses?

    (total monthly expenses) / (gross profit per unit) = # of unit sales needed per month to break even

To illustrate, let's take the example of Luke, a handyman and green-building enthusiast who currently works as a store manager for a retail chain. Luke is considering launching LukeSaver.com, a business to provide small contractors and DIY homeowners with green-building materials such as highly energy-efficient windows, doors, and insulation products. He's planning to operate the business entirely online using the popular affiliate business model—he'll market a carefully curated list of green-building products (sold by big-box stores and manufacturers) to his target customers, and when someone clicks through to a vendor's site (e.g., Pella Windows, Marvin Doors, Home Depot, etc.) to purchase a given product, LukeSaver will collect an affiliate sales commission. His business has very little overhead, since it only markets the products, and has no expenses associated with product development, nor for manufacturing, inventorying, or shipping.

Luke figures that the items purchased on his site (windows, doors, etc.) will carry an average price tag per item of $250. From interviewing a number of DIY homeowners and contractors, he further estimates that the average purchase through his site will be for four items, or a total of $1,000 per purchase. Finally, while affiliate sales commissions can range from 4 percent to 15 percent or higher depending on the vendor and the item, Luke is conservatively assuming his average commission will be 6 percent.

Given this background, Luke's monthly reverse income statement calculation looks like this:

- monthly expenses:
  - salary (just for Luke—no additional staff needed): $8,000 per month
  - benefits (conservative estimate): $2,000
  - overhead (principally marketing, since no rent required): $2,000
  - costs for inventory, shipping, and so on: $0
  - total monthly expenses: $12,000
- gross profit per customer sale:
  - average sale = (four items) × ($250 per item) = $1,000 per customer sale
  - average affiliate commission = 6 percent
  - average affiliate sales commission per customer sale = (6 percent) × ($1,000) = $60
- break-even calculation (i.e., how many customer sales does Luke need to have each month to cover his costs?):
    (monthly expenses of $12,000) / ($60 per customer sale) = 200 customer sales per month

So while Luke can see himself launching LukeSaver as a side-hustle project initially, he aspires to eventually quit his day job and support himself through his startup. Using this simple calculation, he now has a concrete sense as to how realistic that might be, by answering the question "How quickly can he scale up the business to be transacting an average of at least two hundred customer sales per month?" Once he exceeds that threshold on a consistent basis, he can realistically consider working on the business full-time (drawing a salary and benefits from the startup).

TIPS

- The spirit of the reverse income statement is to give you a rough approximation of how big your business would need to be to support your salary and benefits. So avoid false precision; for instance, there's no need to gather multiple quotes for health insurance. A back-of-the-envelope calculation gives you all the information you need during initial planning to gauge whether your startup idea could support you eventually and, if so, when.

RED FLAGS

- A reverse income statement is a useful tool for entrepreneurs contemplating producing and selling a product or service for a certain price. It's less useful for startups such as apps, social networks, or blogs that are predicated on providing a free service in order to build up a large following.

VII

CAPITAL

Capital is another word for money that you or others invest in a business in order to launch it and make it grow. The following is the most important question to consider regarding startup capital as well as a straightforward way to address it.

CHAPTER 19

Is Outside Funding Appropriate, and from Whom Would You Raise It?

As you're evaluating your startup idea, it's useful to develop a sense for whether you should aspire to raise outside funding, and if so, what types of funding sources might consider your business to be a viable investment. Exhibit O shows the Startup Fundability Matrix, a conceptual framework that can provide you with preliminary answers to these questions.

The X (horizontal) axis of the Startup Fundability Matrix indicates capital efficiency, ranging from low to high (left to right). All other things being equal, outside investors prefer to invest their money in businesses that are capital efficient, meaning that for

Exhibit O

THE STARTUP FUNDABILITY MATRIX*

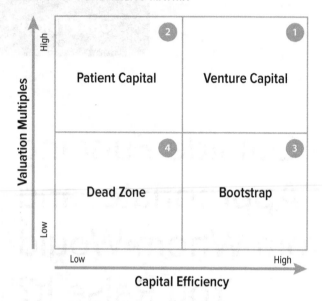

every dollar invested in the business, it's good at producing strong returns for the investors on a dollar-for-dollar basis. On this scale, the businesses that tend to be more appealing to investors—the capital-efficient ones—are those that (a) require a modest amount of capital to launch and/or (b) can be scaled or grown dramatically and efficiently with the injection of a modest level of additional capital.

The Y (vertical) axis of the Startup Fundability Matrix gives a range of valuation multiples, from low to high (bottom to top). Valuation is the value of the company, or its overall financial worth to investors (indicated, for example, by the combined value of a company's total outstanding shares when it goes public or by the purchase price of the company when it is acquired by another). Since the

---

*   The Startup Fundability Matrix is derived from concepts originally described by Professors Timothy L. Faley, PhD, and Peter Adriaens, PhD, in lecture materials in 2012.

shares of a new startup are illiquid—that is, they cannot be bought and sold on a public exchange—it can be challenging to determine their present or future value. Consequently, early-stage investors look at patterns across many companies.

One commonly used pattern or metric is the valuation multiple—that is, how much certain types of companies are typically worth, measured as a multiple of the last twelve months' earnings (profit) or revenue (total sales). To determine these ratios for a publicly traded company, take its market capitalization (the share price times the total number of shares outstanding) and divide that amount by the past year's earnings (to get an "earnings multiple") or revenue (to calculate a "revenue multiple"). When companies are acquired by other companies, the overall purchase price can be divided by earnings or revenue to calculate the same ratios. In business parlance, we say that a company is "valued at 8.5× earnings" (8.5 times the last twelve months' earnings or the last fiscal year's earnings), or perhaps "10× revenue" (ten times the last twelve months' total sales).

In general, businesses that achieve high valuation multiples are those that show (or have potential for) three characteristics: high growth potential, sustainably high profitability, and strong differentiation versus competitors.

Now that you understand the axes of the Startup Fundability Matrix, let's look at what types of businesses fit in which categories.

Quadrant #1 (Upper Right)—Venture Capital

Quadrant #1 businesses have a combination of high valuation multiples (high growth, high profit, and high differentiation) and high scalability—that is, once the company is launched, modest amounts of incremental capital investment have the potential to trigger dramatic company growth. Highly scalable businesses are going after a large addressable market *and* have an easily scalable business model. For instance, a new personal services firm (think consulting, accounting, or executive coaching) may be going after a large addressable market, but the business model is not highly scalable. (To grow your business beyond the capacity of your existing staff, you have to laboriously recruit, hire, train, and grow new consultants with comparable expertise.) By contrast, a cloud-based software business going after a large market (say, in customer relationship management) has a highly scalable business model, since you don't have to invest a lot of money or time in additional "production capacity" in order to add and service additional paying customers.

Typical types of Quadrant #1 businesses include enterprise software companies, social networking apps, technology infrastructure businesses, and medical device startups.

Because of their combination of high multiples and cost-efficient scaling potential, they're the types of startups that appeal to venture capital investors (VCs) and angel investors (high-net-worth individuals).

Quadrant #2 (Upper Left)—Patient Capital

Businesses landing in the second quadrant share the high valuation multiples of Quadrant #1 companies, characterized by a combination of high growth, high profit, and high differentiation. However, companies in Quadrant #2 are less capital efficient. Once launched, they tend to be more difficult to scale rapidly with additional capital, usually due to limited market size. Consequently, investors will tend to see lower potential returns on invested capital than they might from Quadrant #1 companies.

Typical types of Quadrant #2 startups include niche software companies, niche technology companies, and most app businesses.

Their modest market size and lower long-run growth trajectories make them less appealing investments for VCs and many angels. Therefore, these businesses are well advised to pursue more patient capital sources for startup financing, such as specific angel investors showing a special affinity for their particular business sector, friends and family, corporate strategic partners in their industry, federal government grant programs, and local, regional, or state economic development agencies.

Quadrant #3 (Lower Right)—Bootstrap

Third-quadrant startups rank relatively poorly on the scale of valuation multiples. On the other hand, they have the benefit of being relatively capital efficient, in the sense that they tend to require a modest amount of capital to get up and running and generating positive cash flow month to month. Think of Quadrant #3 companies as cash-flow businesses—or as lifestyle businesses.

Startups that fit into Quadrant #3 include personal services businesses, specialty retail ventures, restaurants and bars, niche manufacturing, and the building trades. If, for instance, you're launching a guitar shop—offering new and used instrument sales, repair, and music lessons—you can start such a business with only modest initial investment and operate on a cash-positive basis almost from the outset; a nice and rewarding business to own and operate, but the combination of limited growth potential and poor valuation multiples makes it unappealing to most outside investors. Similarly with a plumbing business or a boutique consultancy: they are relatively inexpensive to launch, rewarding to own and run, but not great investment vehicles for outsiders.

Founders of Quadrant #3 lifestyle businesses tend to launch in "bootstrap" mode by investing personal savings and using personal debt, credit cards, and possibly loans from friends and family or from local economic development agencies. Once you have a successful operating history, you may be able to qualify for a line of credit (LOC) from a bank or a small-business loan. (Always be sure to only borrow amounts you're confident you can repay from operating cash flow.)

Quadrant #4 (Lower Left)—Dead Zone

We call Quadrant #4 the "Dead Zone" because businesses here are extraordinarily difficult for entrepreneurs to finance—and for good reason. They have the deadly combination of poor valuation multiples (low growth, narrow profits, and limited differentiation) and poor capital efficiency (very expensive both to get up and running and to scale).

Typical types of Quadrant #4 businesses include commodity man-ufacturing (say, windows or cement), commodity distribution (i.e., a distributor for restaurant supplies), and undifferentiated or com-modity retail (think groceries, lumber, or office supplies).

These sorts of businesses might be decent to own once they're fully operational. Unfortunately, they tend to require extraordinary amounts of capital to initially build and launch, and once operational, they generate narrow profit margins (due to the commodity nature of the products). Because of this profile, it's extraordinarily difficult to find outside investors interested in funding the startup of a Quad-rant #4 business. Consequently, these businesses are poor choices for entrepreneurs (unless they come to the party with significant amounts of personal capital that they're willing to invest in a busi-ness with limited upside).

 TIPS

- Start by categorizing your startup business on the Y (vertical) axis.
- Generally speaking, technology or tech-enabled businesses tend to rank higher on the Y axis (valuation multiple scale) than do low-tech or no-tech businesses.
- If you think your business ranks highly on the Y axis, the pri-mary determinant of whether you're in Quadrant #2 or #1 is market size. Narrow or niche markets or single-product busi-nesses push a company to the left (Quadrant #2), while very large addressable markets and broader product platforms will push a company to the right (Quadrant #1).
- If your business ranks low on the Y axis, the principle factor pushing you left or right on the matrix is launch cost. Com-panies that can be launched efficiently with a modest amount of capital fall into Quadrant #3, Bootstrap, while those that require large amounts of capital to build (e.g., to fund the

construction of a factory or large store and to purchase large amounts of inventory) fall into Quadrant #4, Dead Zone.

RED FLAGS

- Be clearheaded, and avoid wishful thinking. For instance, low-tech and brick-and-mortar businesses tend to rank low on the Y axis for valuation multiples.
- If you're considering starting a business that would be competing against a multibillion-dollar, established competitor or competitors, that's a clue that you could be looking at a mature market with commodity products and narrow profit margins (i.e., a Quadrant #4, Dead Zone, business).

VIII

THE TEAM

Just as real estate pros list the three most important deal consider-ations as "location, location, location," it's common among veteran entrepreneurs and venture investors to cite the top three startup suc-cess factors as "the team, the team, the team." Obviously, they don't discount the importance of addressing the first nineteen Focal Points of the Launch Lens. But at the end of the day, most investors will tell you they'd always prefer a B-list idea with an A-list team than the other way around. Fundamentally, this is for two reasons:

1. Strong, consistent execution is paramount to the success of any startup.
2. Things will inevitably change during the launch and scaling of a startup, and strong managers are better equipped to pivot and adjust.

CHAPTER 20

Do You Have the Right Team?

Will this business leverage the skills and business competencies of the founding team?

This question applies equally well to entrepreneurial startups as it does to corporate new-business launches. Entrepreneurs need to ask themselves, Is this something I'll enjoy and be good at? For instance, if the business will entail extensive face-to-face interaction with consumers, is that something that you're good at and that you'll truly enjoy? Or if the business will entail organizing and managing myriad details every day, is that something that someone on the founding team is truly gifted at doing and will enjoy?

For corporate startups, this question applies in a different but equally important way. Does the new-business concept take advantage of the organization's established capabilities? For instance, if an industrial corporation that sells its goods primarily through distributors is contemplating launching a new series of branded consumer products, one would have to ask if the founding organization and its executives have the core competencies to do an excellent job of launching such a business. Shouldn't they seek new-business opportunities that have a better strategic fit with their competency profile?

Getting a "No" answer to this Launch Lens question does *not* necessarily mean that your new-business concept is a poor one. Indeed, it may be superb on every other count. But a poor core-competency fit should give you pause. That doesn't necessary mean you should walk away from the opportunity. It may mean, if you are an entrepreneur or startup team, that you need to augment your team with additional people with skills that complement your own. In a corporate startup situation, you may need to either realistically look at new outside hires who add critical skills to the team and/or consider strategic alliances with other companies whose skills complement those of your organization—for instance, perhaps your firm may design and produce the product, and your partner has excellent channel strengths.

TIPS

- Seek to surround yourself with people whose backgrounds and skills complement yours. The best teams have diversity of background, experience, and perspective.
- Strong leaders build teams of "A-list" people with complementary talents and skills, and they are not threatened by them. A good team ought to have one or more individuals who could potentially step in for the CEO. (By contrast, weaker leaders will often surround themselves with "B-list" or "C-list" people who don't threaten them and tend to be "yes-people" rather than active contributors.)

RED FLAGS

- New industry—If you're contemplating launching a startup business in an industry in which you—or you and your partners—have no background, watch out. There are enough risks associated with entrepreneurship. (Can we deliver a product that performs as advertised? Will enough customers buy at a price point that provides us with sufficient profit? Can we reach customers cost efficiently? Can we find sufficient financing?) Think very carefully before you compound those risks—and that learning curve effect—by entering a market with which you're unfamiliar. A better path may be to explore entrepreneurial opportunities in an industry in which you've already got some experience and contacts and know the lay of the land.

- Homogeneous founding team—If your founding team comprises two or more individuals with very similar backgrounds and training, that can be problematic. Seek background diversity on your team.

Conclusion

Applying the Launch Lens

Now that you've got a keen grasp on the twenty Focal Points of the Launch Lens framework, the following page (Exhibit P) provides you with a worksheet that you can copy and use as a tool for articulating, comparing, screening, and communicating *your* new-business ideas. And remember, applying the Launch Lens is a process, not an event. You can start with a quick, twenty-minute screen without any research— simply your best guesses. If your idea seems to pass that first muster, the next step might be to dedicate a few hours to quickly researching and validating (or disproving and revising) your initial working hypothesis. Ultimately, if your idea is something that proves worth pursuing further, the Launch Lens gives you an invaluable framework for developing a more detailed business plan for your business.

And through it all, remember the advice of President Dwight D. "Ike" Eisenhower: "Plans are nothing. Planning is everything." How do we apply Ike's thinking to our lives as entrepreneurs? We're not looking for one right answer to any of these questions but rather answers that, individually and taken together, form a strong working hypothesis. The facts—and our assumptions—will change over time. But meanwhile, we'll never regret having taken a rigorous, systematic approach to planning—to asking the right questions.

LAUNCH LENS WORKSHEET © JIM PRICE

Your name:

Startup business name:

One-sentence description:

	The Launch Lens: *20-Question Entrepreneurship Framework*	Answers for Your Startup Business
Problem	1. Who are your customers?	
	2. What is your customers' unmet need?	
	3. How are your customers addressing this need today?	
Solution	4. What is your solution?	
	5. How will your customers benefit?	
Market	6. How big is your market?	

(*continued*)

	The Launch Lens: *20-Question Entrepreneurship Framework*	Answers for Your Startup Business
	7. Which customer segments will you target and why?	
	8. Who are your competitors, and how do you compare?	
Business model	9. How will your business make money?	
	10. How will you price your product?	
	11. Which functions will you perform in-house vs. outsource?	
	12. How scalable is your business?	
Marketing and sales	13. How will you gather customer input?	

(continued)

The Launch Lens: *20-Question Entrepreneurship Framework*	Answers for Your Startup Business
14. How will your customers acquire your product?	
15. How will you promote to your customers?	
Finance 16. How much will it cost to launch the business?	
17. Can the business generate sustainably high profits?	
18. At what point could you quit your day job?	
Capital 19. Is outside funding appropriate, and from whom would you raise it?	
Team 20. Do you have the right team?	

Index

Page numbers followed by *t* refer to tables.

About the Author

Jim Price is a serial tech entrepreneur and business educator. For several years, he's held a position on the entrepreneurial studies faculty at the University of Michigan's Ross School of Business, where he also serves as an entrepreneur in residence at the Zell Lurie Institute for Entrepreneurial Studies (zli.umich.edu).

Over the past two-plus decades, Jim has launched and led—as CEO/founder/chairman—multiple tech-enabled startups, and has had the good fortune of having been a part of two successful company sales and an IPO. He continues to serve as an advisor and board member to multiple startups while also consulting for Global 2000 companies on the successful launch of internal tech startups and spinouts.

A Stanford MBA, father of two, and lifelong musician, Jim has lived on both coasts but now happily resides in the college town and vibrantly entrepreneurial community of Ann Arbor, Michigan. He describes startup variety as his brain food, mentoring as his golf, and coffee-shop chaos as his peace.

Follow the author on Twitter @jimpricestartup or follow his writings and philosophy at www.jimpricestartup.com.